FINDING YOURSELF

For Starseeds and Lightworkers

Activations from 7 Star Races for Reawakening to Your Galactic Presence

by the Galactic Team for Earth Starseed Reactivation and Support

Brought to Earth by Gil Sim

Finding YourSELF for Starseeds and Lightworkers
Copyright © 2019 by Gil Sim

E-mail: info@cosmic-light-human.com
Website: http://www.cosmic-light-human.com

ISBN: 9781091875197
First Edition

Contents

Acknowledgements *from* **Gil Sim**

A special thanks goes to all the people who have made this body of work possible.

To my parents, for providing a conducive space where I may focus on this body of work.

To Robin Morlock, for helping with refining the spellings of the names of each of the 7 star races in this book.

To all my guides and angels, who have been prompting me to get this book done at record speed (20 days!) and who have provided huge forward momentum for this project.

To the country of Singapore where I live, which has provided the excellent infrastructure in terms of internet and logistics connectivity needed to distribute these downloads quickly and efficiently from the galactic committees onward to the rest of the globe.

Note to The Reader

The contents of this book were specially designed and put together by the Galactic Team for Earth Starseed Support. This is a galactic committee that is located very close to Earth in alignment with its function of overseeing the activation, functioning and support of Earth Starseeds. The committee works closely with each Starseed that is presently on the Earth plane and is presently (as of March 2019) concerned primarily with awakening Starseeds to their planetary missions. This is a matter of some urgency to the committee, which sees that a large number of Earth Starseeds presently feel confused and lost as to what they have contracted to do on Earth. The book serves as a reminder and reactivation call to Starseeds, encouraging each to discover the answers that are already embedded inside of themselves.

Gil Sim works together with the committee to deliver tools for self-discovery to Earth Starseeds. This book is brought directly from the committee down to Earth with Gil providing the direct channel and transcription of the material onto the physical plane. The committee takes responsibility for all of the material in the book and notes and keeps for future reference all feedback provided by readers as these thoughts and vibrations are generated on the etheric realms as the reader goes through the book. Gil is also taking and welcomes feedback on the physical plane from readers who would like to provide their views.

Foreword

by the Galactic Team for Earth Starseed Reactivation and Support on the Purpose of this Book

Greetings! If you are here, you are probably excited at what is in the book, and what you may find that will tickle you, awaken you, touch you, and remind you of what it is that you are here for. Because being on Earth has not always been the easiest of things. Earth can be harsh. Earth can be cruel. Earth can be unsympathetic. It can feel as if Earth has no place for you. And it can often feel that way, all of these things together.

You sometimes wonder – why should I care? Why should I care anymore? Nothing I do is acceptable here, the real truth of who I am, what I want to do, what I stand for, what I want to speak out about – all of these are not welcome! I can either stand for myself in vain, drowned out by voices of ridicule, put-down, judgment at who I am, and finally go back all alone having accomplished nothing except accumulating a pile of wounds from having been hurt so much by the others who don't understand. Or I can simply accept that this is the way that it is, and give up all hope, because change is futile. And live out the rest of my days in silence, feeling alone, hating this world for all that it is, for all that it is not, never believing that it will amount to anything other than what it is today, yesterday, and for the last couple of thousand years.

We bring good news however. Yes, Earth has been in an epoch of dense cruelty, barbarity, and disconnection for a period of time. This is true. And, there is a way out. This way involves you.

You. Yes you. What do you mean me? You might ask. No, no, no, I can't be the answer or solution to anything. I am too small, too meagre, too weak, too damaged, too hurt. Me? Me? What does "Me" have to do with anything on this planet? I can't do anything.

People won't listen to me. People aren't interested in what I have to say. I am not big enough to be taken seriously and paid attention to.

That's only what you think, we tell you. You have no idea. Why do you even believe what you believe about yourself, have you ever wondered? What has caused you to shrink so small from your original aspirations and grandeur? What have you absorbed from the beliefs and opinions of others that has caused your aura to contract? Get rid of them. They are not you. They are not yours to carry. Start connecting back with who you are. For you are a starseed, a powerful lightworker, a soul who has come to earth to be of galactic service. Inside of you somewhere, you already know this. It is time that you own up to this, and take your rightful place as someone who has come here to shift things, to transform things, to help raise humanity up to its next transcendent levels.

The Reason You Came that you are Re-Remembering

Many eons ago, as a galactic soul, you made a commitment to be of service. Many many star races in the galaxy have come together to make this commitment. It was a commitment to be in charge of different tasks, different aspects of a collective mission and purpose to assist the Earth in her next evolution. It was at that time that many of you chose either to take on roles superintending different aspects of Earth's development, including through incarnations on Earth to introduce new ideas, concepts, energies here, or even to create events that would change the course of Earth's history of development. Many of you on Earth have done this over the course of the multiple incarnations that you have had here, relentlessly pursuing the same mission through a period of time. Collectively, we are grateful for your service. We recognize how challenging this was for many of you, and the sacrifices and sufferings that accumulated as a by-product of your mission accomplishment. Many of you continue to carry these burdens, these old scars, these old hurts…and the walls and defenses that you have built around them in order to even just stay alive and keep functioning. We are grateful and immensely appreciative of all that you are carrying and have carried in order to accomplish your tasks. And in this day and age, we say to you – there is no more need to carry these old burdens.

We are at a point now in history where the light is coming into Earth at an unprecedented rate. And where the light shines, it disinfects, it releases, it brings awareness to what you have had to carry through the ages so that you may finally shed it all off. All of it, yes. Allow these to gently peel off you. Let the light do its work. And receive the light with gratitude, commitment, and powerful might.

There is an opportunity now for each and every single one of you to rise up into love, into gentleness, into hope, joy, beauty and eyes of softness for the world again. As you shed off what has burdened you, this is what awaits you. More than this, there is an opportunity for you to take charge of your life, to take charge of what goes on in the world, to rise into your power to change things for the better for all – now, and for many of the future generations to come.

The Reason for This Book

This book has been placed on Earth and brought to you by the Galactic Team for the Coordination, Reawakening and Healing of all Starseeds on the planet Earth. We place this here as our way of letting you know that far from being forgotten, we have constantly been working to support and assist you. Since the moment you stepped onto Earth, we have been keeping track of your progress, of your mission, of your well-being, and we have kept logs on what we can do to help move you forward. These logs have kept us informed of the general state of everyone on Earth, and what additional elements that you need in order to be able to perform your missions more effectively. They have enabled us to constantly update our plans for Starseed support and to bring all of you different downloads and healing energies as needed. They also inform us of how much each of you has suffered, and the suffering that you need healing for as a collective group. We fully empathize with each and every single one of you. Be assured that customized plans continue to be developed for the support of each individual Starseed on planet Earth.

We are working with Gil at this time to deliver downloads, packages of care, and activations to each and every single one of you. Gil is part of us and superintends the distribution of energies of care and support for Earth Starseeds. She is bringing through this book as part of her life's mission – similar to the individual missions that each of you will be waking up to, once we can get our communications and messages through to you more effectively. The missions are already there, yes, and it is really a matter of you being able to allow them to emerge from the deepest-most parts of your being – your soul.

This book is filled with wonderful activations, wisdom teachings and energies from 7 star races who have taken on the agreement to assist with the reawakening and reactivation of Starseeds such as you. Each of the 7 races has contributed deep and potent gifts and techniques that are embedded inside of the text of the book. They bring this to you and offer it to you so that you may remember all of your light again, and be a powerful light on this planet. You do not have to be anything other than who you really are – and reawakening to this, fully accepting and knowing this IS the key to your fullest light. Challenging sometimes, yes. Because so much of society has told you that you are unacceptable when you do this, and that, when you be this, and that, such that it has become a learned habit almost for you to disguise every single thing that you are to fit into an artificial construct defined by society for who it thinks you need to be. Almost like a robot – defined for a function, yet lacking in free will, emotion, self-expression, unconventionality, inspired creativity – in other words all that makes a human soul shine as itself this world.

Chuck that all away! We tell you. Chuck away every single thing that you believe that you need to be to get accepted by your society and by this world. It is not necessary. You are really perfect as you are, even yes with all the things you consider imperfections. The holes in yourself you think need to be plugged, the stuff that needs fixing, the places where you are 'not enough'. Look deeper into those places. Hear their message. Because they are the key to your rising up.

Look at their light! What looks like a weakness is sometimes your greatest strength, your greatest humanity, your greatest wisdom! They are in you for a reason, for they can tell powerful stories that inspire others to courage, tears, and conviction for changing the world. They inspire others to relay the message behind their pain, the wisdom that has resulted from it, and the healing that needs to continue – not just for you but for all others who have been similarly afflicted in the world. They create understanding, fortitude, and above all, convictions that will lead you on the path towards the accomplishment of your mission.

Accepting yourself is the key to finding yourself – to finding ALL of who and what you are. No ifs, no buts, it is about finding and gathering back every single piece of you throughout all space and time, putting it all back together, and saying unequivocally – this is me, and it is a fact, simple as that. And being able to say this with detachment, a transcendent perspective, and the openness to allowing all of yourself to evolve into its next iterations. Everything changes – the Universe is always changing as a constant – and so will you change too. It is not about not allowing change. It is about creating the firm foundations for the next iterations of change to emerge, like how a plant emerges from a seed and thanks the seed for being who it is that has allowed the plant to blossom forth.

So take this message, and remember it as the foundation that will enable you to get the most out of the downloads embedded in the rest of this book. The rest of this book waters the seed that has already been placed in your hands energetically as you read the text above. This is the seed that will spread through your energy field, tunneling into places and spaces inside of you to break up stagnant energies, open them up to the light, and create space for receiving new energies that are already waiting to come into you once the old has been emptied out. Expect to be transformed, expect new sensations, consciousnesses and discoveries to arise to the fore. It is a total transformation of your energy field that we are intending with this book, and each of you will receive as much as you are able to at the present time, as you are willing to.

So enjoy, and we give this book to you with our very warmest blessings, for it is part of our purpose to ensure that each of you succeeds – and not just succeeds but succeeds magnificently – as a galactic soul in human form, moving forward with all that you have intended in your incarnation.

Please proceed with the rest of this book, through each of the chapters. Preferably in order, as there is a certain sequence to receiving the activations. And of course, if you wish to receive certain activations more strongly, you may always choose to re-read specific chapters that call out in particular to you. Each chapter contains powerful downloads that shake up your energy field and go into deep spaces and places inside of your soul.

With all our blessings,

The Galactic Coordination Team for Earth Starseed Reactivation and Support

Chapter 1

Keys to Processing Your Human Experience

To begin with, let's go into an overview of Earth's place in the galaxy, and the reasons for the special interest in Earth.

Earth's Role in the Galaxy

Earth occupies a special place in the galaxy. It is where many races have come together as a melting pot – if you will, contributing our gifts, traits and special energies into the formation of human DNA across time. As star races, we have done this because of our love for creation, our love for blending different types of energies together into ever richer forms that express the full glory of our Prime Creator. Our Prime Creator watches over and experiences each of these forms as him/her/itself, taking pride and pleasure in each of these new experiences.

As children of the Prime Creator, we the star races too have our own creative impulses. We have the desire to seed. We have the desire to watch as our seeds grow, and to help nourish and develop our own creations into their next evolutionary forms. We do this as an extension of our being children of the Prime Creator, as we have the Prime Creator inside of us.

The Chaotic Process of Enriching Creation

At times, our creations – the people that we have given birth to – take on personalities and characteristics that we may find unfamiliar to ourselves. A mutation, so to speak. Mutations are new forms emerging. They may look and feel different, and seem to not fit, and they are also new opportunities for growth of an entire species. They carry new messages, new realizations, new challenges to an existing order that have the potential to carry what is currently in the present to a higher, elevated level. They carry the force for change. World change. Transformational change. Organizational change. Earth change. They are here to challenge everyone and everything to rise up and seek a new way that embraces a richer diversity that integrates differences into a higher level of functioning. They take two plus two and make five, where we never imagined that five was possible. They create a quantum leap out of existing logic into new possibilities that we never envisioned for ourselves before – until these beings that we sometimes view as mutations come along.

What does this have to do with you on Earth, with us watching Earth, and all of what has happened in the galaxy? The short and simple answer is that this IS our history – our collective history. Throughout all time, we have been one, and then many, in an increasing order of greater variety. We have seeded new races. We have then become those new races. And you have then chosen to be and experience those new races, in many different ways. In your current incarnation, you have made the choice to experience the richness of being a human being, the product of many generations of seeding and reseeding by different types of star races all across the galaxy.

How does this concern you now? You may ask. I'm stuck here, in this human form that I find distasteful, disgusting (to some of you), and eminently fallible and weak. This form is frail. It lasts maybe what – 70-90 years? And then it decays, and it becomes horrible. Why would anyone want to be in this thing? Me? Least of all. What point did this ever serve? Eugh. I can't wait to get out. Take me out, take me out, take me away, back home home home!

To this we say, your being here is the product of an empowered choice that you made before incarnation. It was an empowered choice to experience certain types of energies for learning, for enriching the knowledge of your soul, and for service to the Earth community. You wanted to come, and the point is to wake up to what it is you intended for yourself when you chose to. The avoidance of your human path is never the solution. Embracing the reasons for it that you know in your heart of hearts is the truth is the key to a joyful and meaningful life here. And this is a key that is available to every single one of you, now more so than ever before in the history of humankind on the planet.

The Keys to the Base Coding (i.e. the DNA) of Humanity

Take advantage of this key. It is being handed to you right now as we speak, and as you read through this text. This key will show you into the library of your DNA base coding, where there lies a shelf with books on your incarnational experience as a human being. In these books lie all the higher purposes and meanings of every single one of your experiences as a soul as it relates to your human consciousness. Take this key, unlock the library, go to your shelf, and read through the books that are about you. They will tell you all about the reasons behind why you have gone through what you have been through, and futures that they point towards, having planted seeds already in your experience for things to unfold, blossom and ripen.

(Note to Readers from Gil: DNA here refers to Deoxyribonucleic Acid, the scientific name for the hereditary material in human beings that contains the instructions for building a life form. Science has discovered two strands of DNA in the physical cells of each person that gives them their physical

characteristics such as height, hair color, and health. In actual fact, human DNA is much more than that – it is a vast multi-dimensional library of information that contains all the experiences as well as instructions for the awakening and transformation of an individual consciousness through its multiple forms and evolutions throughout time. As of the time of writing – March 2019 – the multi-dimensional DNA library for all of humanity is opening up and connecting in a massive way to the rest of the cosmos outside of Earth. In the next section, you are presented with the key to the room in this multi-dimensional library that contains your own individual DNA.)

Instructions for Using the Key

Take heed for how to use the key that you have just been given.

1. First, place yourself in a comfortable position where you will be free of distractions. Turn off the radio, your mobile phone, close the door, and place yourself in a space where you can be fully with yourself for the next half an hour or so.

2. Once you are in position, imagine yourself walking towards a door – the entrance towards the room where you will find all of the files on your DNA base coding. This room contains every single thing in your DNA – every single experience, choice, thought, feeling, person you have encountered in your consciousness as a human. In this room, there are files that call out to you to be aware of them, and also some that jump out at you to be read.

3. Choose one of the files that are jumping out are you to indicate that they want to be read at this time. These are high priority files that are urgently wanting your attention. They

are here to reveal to you information that is of particular importance to you at this time – new awareness about yourself that is buried deep inside of your DNA. They are here to reveal what is true about you to you, so that you may recognize deeper layers of yourself that you had never been able to put your finger to previously. "Ahh…. ! I see now what that was all about! Ahh… I now understand the reason I am the way I am, the reason I did that earlier on in my life, and the reason certain things in my life were arranged the way they were." These are the types of realizations and aha-s that these files are holding for you.

This is a precious room, for it contains every single one of your experiences as a human being. It IS your base coding that is inside of your DNA, i.e. inside of you. It IS you. Meaning that, it contains not only all that you have experienced, but also all that is your potential to become. Many of these files are lighting up at the present time, now, waiting to come alive again, and to reveal even more about you to yourself. They are waiting to jog your memory to what you have forgotten about yourself – the remembrances and genes that have gone dark inside of your base coding, that are operating in a soft murmur in the background. These are all waiting to rev-up again, bringing their traits, gifts, and energies back into your being and everyday life on the planet. Welcome them back into your life with gratitude for their return. Embrace the new uncomfortable-ness that they bring through shifting you to a different way of doing and being. Work with them to create and allow the changes to happen in your waking life.

The key has been placed within this book for your use. Use it well, and wisely. It will work with you to awaken DNA inside of you gradually over time, in batches and in a sequence that is most appropriate to you. Thank the key, and keep it inside of your field. It will be with you from this point forth, for as long as you want to have it in your field.

The Purpose behind Giving You the Keys

And now, we speak more about the purpose of this key. For many eons, humanity has not had the opportunity to consciously manage and control its own evolution. This key to your own base coding has been withheld from you. It has been withheld from you, because you would have entered your base coding and fiddled with the files from a state of gross ego. Imagine what damage you would have done to yourselves! Imagine mauling your own DNA, which is what many of you would have inadvertently done, from a state of unconsciousness. It is for that reason that these keys have been kept hidden away, tucked in places and spaces that you could not have found until a certain level of consciousness had emerged inside of the human experience.

And now, many on the planet are reaching the level of consciousness where you are capable of being with this key in a manner that is responsible. You are capable now of entering the room of your own base coding, of knowing the sacredness of this room, and of treating all of your experiences as recorded in the files with respect and reverence. You are wise enough to be able to take ownership of this key and make conscious use of it.

And this is the reason that the key has been handed over to you at this time. It is time now for you to take charge of your own base coding, it is time for you to participate consciously in the development of your DNA. You own your own room with all your DNA files. How would you like this room to be like? What kind of energies do you want to cultivate and grow in there? How do you want your DNA to blossom? What would you like to read first, and work on first? Inside of your personal DNA library, the choices are yours to make, and your DNA responds to all of your choices and decisions. You can either ignore what is there, or you can set an intention of becoming consciously aware, bit by bit, of the files that are stored inside.

Enjoy the exploration of your own base coding, and we wish you all the best with working with your own DNA to create your own evolutionary path.

And now we turn back to you as a human being on Earth, that many of you have so much discomfort with that you are calling out to get out!

Using the Keys to Find Your Purposes and Mission(s)

With this key, you no longer have to suffer the whys of being here that you have many times in your life cried out for as a painful existential question. You can explore your DNA libraries/files, for all of the answers regarding you as a human consciousness are in there.

Read your files, and understand the reason(s) you are here. With this knowing, much of your suffering will dissipate, as you **get** on a deeper level the missions you have undertaken to do and start understanding your life experiences as the pathways that lead you towards being able to complete these missions effectively. Go now, and do this. Start with the book on your present lifetime. Let the contents of the book pour out to you, speaking of all the pain that you have experienced, all those times you felt angry, alone, victimized by the world. Let the book then show you where all of this is taking you towards, the trajectory that this has created for your life. See yourself becoming, blossoming from all of this pain, making you who you are that becomes the person-being uniquely suited to the mission you have come here for.

Using the Keys to Explore Your Galactic Origins

And then, if you have time and space, turn to the next book that tells you of your star origins. This is the book that will explain the context behind your decision to take up incarnation on Earth, and the realities of the mission that you have come to accomplish. This book can tell you a lot about your primary orientation and drive across all lifetimes.

As you read your books, genetic coding that has been buried for a long time comes alive. When you bring your awareness to your genetic history, the space opens for it to morph and evolve into its next level of function. As you read, this is what you are doing – you are bringing attention and awareness to what is calling out for attention, enabling it to shift, to release its pain, and to develop into its next stage of blossoming.

In the next chapter, we will speak more about getting to know yourself, finding yourself, and being you as your soul on Earth.

Chapter 2

Being as a Galactic Soul on Earth

WWhen you incarnated on Earth, you came as a soul and chose a human form. You were ensouled on the 3-dimensional physical plane, a multidimensional being projecting part of yourself into 3-dimensional physical matter. You pellestrated into this form that you now consider rather limited in functionality (it can't fly, nor run very fast, or swim without breathing, or project into outer space). And as you took this form, you started identifying with it over time, believing that it was you, and resenting the limitations that it imposed on your otherwise multi-dimensional self. This is a primary cause of Starseed irritation at the Earth experience – having to squeeze yourself into a form that does not seem able to carry all of you, a form that staples you down to Earth when you would rather be reaching for the stars, exploring the galaxy, and connecting with your star families - a form that feels as if it won't cooperate with everything that you really want to do or have dreamed of doing. Some of you have turned to body-hating ("I hate this body that is now mine that sticks to me like a wart!") and feeling that the sooner that you can leave this incarnation, the better.

We bring you words and energies of consolation at this. We know it has not been easy. And we would like to offer you some presents and gifts. A care package and messages from home, you can think of it as. Messages to let you know that you are cared for still, that your star families continue to keep track of you as you undergo your human experience. Above all, messages that inform you of what you need to do at this time specifically, given all that is going on in the galaxy and on the Earth.

As you read this book, the messages that are meant for you come through in an energetic download. You can think of it as that when you read this book, a conduit opens up that allows us to reach you more easily. You may experience it as a wave of energy coming through to you, or you may hear certain words and messages that are for you specifically, or you may start feeling inklings to do certain things – a sign that the message has been received by subconscious parts of you that are now prompting the conscious parts of you to think differently and take action. The point is, we are working strongly with you to wake you to your calling, to wake you up to who you are, and through this book, the direct channel that runs from us to you strengthens.

So as you read this book, know that there are many different things happening. You are receiving messages from us, and energies to call you up to your mission. You are receiving words of healing and consolation to assist you in being with your Earth experience with greater empowerment, faith in your mission, and optimism for a better humanity. Finally, you are receiving gifts of energies and technologies to open you up to realizing and being the powerful being that you really are.

We present this to you as an unconditional blessing. Yes, you, we present this to you. Receive it with joy. Open yourself to receiving it! Let it unfold inside of you, into all the parts of you that benefit from it. And do know that behind all of this, or perhaps the most critical part of this, is our deep love for you – a love that you may have missed so much, a love that you never felt you could obtain on this planet. For it is a love that is between members of the same soul group who love, cherish and see one another, eye to eye, heart to heart, and soul to soul. Connect with us and feel this love now. Be with this love, and know and enjoy this love. We really do love you to depths that you may not even remember consciously given all that you have been through on planet Earth.

Awareness of your Soul's Journey on Earth

As you read this book, take also the opportunity to reflect on what has been the meaning of your life on Earth. Who has come into your life who has changed it over the course of time here? Who has spoken words that have impacted you? What events in your life, what events in the world have driven you to have strong feelings about the way things should or shouldn't be on this planet? Who has spoken words to you that have caused you to question your opinions, doubt yourself, and put yourself down? And finally, what is it that you feel most strongly about at this time as a cause that you would willingly devote your life to with no qualms at all?

Ponder over these questions, as the answers to them are emerging as you read this book and receive the activations embedded inside the pages. When you get clear about yourself and the things that truly matter in your heart and soul, the world gains a powerful light-seeker and worker who knows the change that they are here to create and becomes savvy and creative about how this is to be done on Earth. We need every single one of you to become this. All of you.

Beginning the Journey back Home

So take this book, and enjoy the activations, exercises, and activities in it. Think of this book as an energetic map that has been given to you to find the promised land of yourself. As you walk the path on the map, you receive clues and triggers that enable you to proceed to the next stages. Treat each chapter seriously, for they contain important messages and teachings that enable you to release all that you are not, to release all your burdens, so you may travel forward lighter, cleaner, freer, ready to meet your own Divine light.

See you in the next chapters, as you begin your journey forward.

Chapter 3

The Activation for Interstellar Communications

The Gift from the Acturians[1]

---

[1] *Note to Readers from Gil: The Acturians are a small faction of the Arcturians that sit away from the main body in order to perform the specialist function of transmitting information and energies all across the galaxy. The slight difference in spelling of the name of this faction distinguishes them from the main Arcturian body. With thanks to Robin Morlock for this insight.*

We are the Acturians. We come from a star system that is 12 trillion light years away from Earth. Yes, you heard right. We are able to travel all over the galaxy and our function here in the context of the Earth mission is to assist Starseeds in getting their inter-stellar communications devices installed and operational in their fields. We have been assisting various individuals in setting up their inter-stellar communications equipment for a period of time now, and it is time for this to be available more widely to everyone on the planet.

The Gift of the Acturians

Within the text of this chapter, we have embedded our gift to you – a download that you may receive to open you up to receiving the specific frequencies and types of communication bursts that your star families and parties within the galactic system with whom you have agreed to coordinate are using for communications with you. This gift allows you receive, decode, and have unfold in your system the energies and messages that assist you in knowing what to do and be in alignment with what you are here on Earth to complete as per your pre-incarnation agreement.

This gift also comes with deeper teachings around ceasing rebellion patterns and surrendering to a higher purpose that your soul has wanted to pursue since the start of your incarnation on Earth. It contains an energy that tells you, "Stop your rebellion NOW, at this instant!" It delivers a firm (and stern) wake-up call to the parts of you that are angrily saying, "No, I won't!" or "Try make me." It tolerates no nonsense, including by delivering a sharp rebuke into your system as needed. This is the firm parent, the mother who shuts you up in the middle of your stories and excuses and tells you to get on with it instead of whining about how hard it is, how you don't want to do it, how impossible it is going to be, how it can't be done. 'No more excuses' is the mantra of this energy.

The Purpose of the Gift

We give this to you because truly what is needed to get things going is for YOU to get going. You are the agent for change. The world is waiting for you to act. When you align with the galactic coordination teams, when you are fully connected to all that is taking place in the galaxy, it becomes easier for you to know what to do and be in any moment. We can then send people to you who are part of your mission, knowing that you can deliver the energies that they need, and receive the energies that they have for you. Your connections with the people with whom you share a common purpose or people who are involved in your purpose strengthen as you receive and use this gift.

Preparation for the Activation – Reflecting within Yourself

Ask yourself now the following:

a) Where am I fearing taking responsibility?

b) Where am I not wanting to believe how much capability I have to be a force for good?

c) Who have I believed who has told me that I can't do it?

Who has ridiculed me, put me down, or in any way tried to quash my faith in my own truths before I have even gotten started?

d) What made me believe them? What made me buy into their stories about me as fact?

e) Where can I be more encouraging toward myself, instead of putting myself down?

f) What kind of support can I give myself to follow, stand up for, and act on my truths every single day?

Take a sheet of paper, reflect on these questions and write down your answers. As you journal, go as deep as you can, and be amazed at what shows up for you. We are here supporting you as you do this exercise, giving you nudges, and holding the space for even more that may or may not be in your current awareness to emerge as realizations.

The Earth Context and Your Role as a Starseed

Be aware of where and how you have bought into the stories of this world, of planet Earth, of human societies on Earth that have often sought to quash those who are different, those who question, those who appear to pose a threat to the existing order, out of a misguided fear for collective survival. Groups often see a threat in new ideas, concepts, or actions that fall outside of their existing frameworks of being and doing that they are not immediately able to interpret or handle. Your task is to realize that this is going on, understand that what you are seeing is an instinctive fear for self-preservation on their part, and to be patient when you perceive that this is what is taking place. Be the ambassador for a new point of view. Wait and hold the space as this new information downloads and integrates into the others in the group. It takes time for new energies to be integrated, and this is true everywhere in the Universe.

As a Starseed, your role in groups is typically to be the one who sees a different or higher perspective. You are the one who looks forward and sees how what everybody is doing today will need to change in order to be ready for the future. Because on an instinctive level, you have already seen the future, you have already seen what is going to come, and the practices of today may make little sense to you or even seem completely crazy from a future-perspective. It is much like, if someone from the future were to arrive back at present-day Earth, he or she might look upon everyone today with the highly-critical eye of a schoolteacher regarding the handiwork of messy, dirty, and barbaric children. This is exactly how you as a Starseed may feel towards the people of today, towards others in groups and communities that you may already be a part of -- whether by choice, by birth, by accident, or by any circumstance.

Your role in groups is to be the schoolteacher. A wise schoolteacher, carrying the energies of patience, firmness, and understanding for where everyone else is at. You do not get angry at children for being children! The children look to you for wisdom that will assist them in their learning. Teach, guide, mentor. Point them towards insights that will light up new realizations for them. Be patient, as they take in new information from your field. They may not always like it, they may react badly at first, and yet, trust that information is being transferred energetically from your consciousness to theirs. On a higher level, their souls are getting what you are transmitting to them when you teach, mentor, and guide them. This is your job. Focus on your job. And ignore the egos that are running amok on the level of the physical plane as people process the new information brought through you. Where new light comes in, that which is in resistance to it arises to be processed and released, and the fact that it does is the natural consequence of you being on mission! So expect it to happen, and this IS you bringing your light to the group and causing the healing to happen!

Exercise patience with those who oppose you. Of course they will. Things have been done this way for centuries, for ages, for a long long time. There is fear that change will cause destruction, where the status quo has generated stability for a long time. People need time to become aware of the cracks in the edifices that they have built and to become convinced that these cracks point to a need for change. Inside of them, they are constantly weighing two sides – will change cause more harm than good? For change is always risky. You don't always know what you are going to get when things change. And sometimes, it can for people feel easier to stick with the devil that they know rather than the angel that they don't.

What You Already ARE Doing and How to Handle it Better

As Starseeds, you bring new frequencies and new types of DNA coding into the energetic matrix of humanity. What does this mean? Well, for one, it means that you will be introducing new thought patterns into the human energy field. New thoughts that disrupt old ones, stopping them in their tracks. Where others are grumbling at things, feeling hopeless and cynical that things won't change, you are the weird person who says, 'Why don't we all do this thing?' Where 'this thing' is something that everyone goes 'huh' at because they've never ever thought about things in this manner. And then they take it in and digest what you've said for a while, and something inside of them changes, something inside of them has shifted to a new angle, even if they may or may not have done what you suggested immediately. You are the person who says, 'We could all just do Y right here right now'. And proceed to lay out an entire visionary plan for the future based on the wildest dreams of what humanity can achieve – plans and dreams that completely blow even your own mind as you are thinking about it and laying it all out. You are the dreamer in the group who fantasizes about huge possibilities, AND staunchly believes they are actually possible, weird as they might seem even to some parts of yourself.

Give people your unique perspective, and allow them to make what they will of it. Because there are always parts that they will find valuable, even if they are not able to reconcile the entirety of it with their existing frames for making sense of and acting in the world. In time to come, they will be able to integrate the valuable energies that you have brought them more and more, and that is where the real shift will happen with them. Your job is not to make this happen, but to play your part in their learning and allow THEM to make the shift for themselves when it is time. For another person's decisions are never your responsibility. Let go of trying to make others who you believe it would be better for them to be. Have faith in their own capacity to understand and make the best choices for themselves independently, with all that they are able to grasp at any moment in time. You do your part, and let them do theirs.

What has all of this to do with inter-stellar communications? You may ask. A lot, is the answer. When you receive energies and messages from us, you may have the tendency to want to distribute and push them onto other people. You are constructed that way as a Starseed, to want to quickly distribute these galactic perspectives and energies to others, to want to 'make' them sit up, take notice, and hey 'get awake now'! You want the best for them, and you do it in the way that you know best, by giving them what we are giving you as information, energies, frequency codes, and other types of energy downloads. And the tendency is to push things onto people. To try to overwhelm and force things onto their patterns that you believe are not serving them so that you can *have your way* with them, where you believe your way is better for them!

Patience Is NEEDED!

And yet, nothing could be further from the truth. When you try to impose your way on others, it stuffs THEM down, it stuffs down their real authentic being. A couple of things could happen as a result.

One, they could get confused. Because what you are telling them conflicts with a genuine part of them that might be thinking and feeling differently, and these pieces of them have a wisdom of their own too. When there is a conflict between two genuine belief systems, massive confusion gets created. Which one do I go with? They might be thinking. Do not burden them with this, because for some people, this is too much for them at this time. It is not a service that you are doing them to throw them into what they are not able to handle.

Two, they go into rebellion. "I absolutely will not tolerate or accept this," they might tell you. "I won't tolerate you." They might say this with a hatred that comes from feeling obliterated as an individuated being by your insistence that they give up their views in favour of yours. For there is nothing more threatening to a person who has misidentified him or herself with their faith, their existing beliefs, their existing views, than being told that everything they believe in is incorrect. It is a full-fledged existential crisis that they will fall into if they do not vigorously attack you back to defend the ego constructs that are operating in their lives. It feels like a survival threat, and their response will reflect those feelings.

Three, they disconnect. They will change the subject entirely because it is too much for them to engage you on the terms that you desire they engage you on. They would rather not face it than encounter what you want to push to them and feel the entire edifice of their beliefs systems crumble apart. Remember that not everyone can handle this amount of destruction of their beliefs systems in such a short time. It needs sometimes to be gentle, slower, with time taken for the entire process of making a 180-degree shift.

Getting YourSELF Across

And then there are those rare souls who get you on a deep soul level instantly. 'Ah.' They might say. And you know instantly that it has triggered a deep realization inside of them. And then they proceed to ponder over your words, letting the new downloads that they have received from you stir inside their system, and their own deeper views on the matter start to emerge from within them. These are the souls you know you can have a deep conversation with immediately, and that the exchange will be productive.

The point is – be gentle on those who do not understand what you are bringing to them because what you are bringing represents a big shock to their system. Yet, never compromise on your truth. The truth is not something that you need to bring across forcefully, or stuff down to somebody else. It is simply you, as who you are, that is conveyed primarily through your way of being. It emanates out of your every pore, regardless of what you are doing, or saying. People get it. On a higher level, people are going to get it because that is the truest communication that is coming out of you to them. It is a communication that supersedes all types of ego defenses that they might put up at words thrown at them unwantedly. It transcends mental understanding and is the most powerful type of communication for this very reason. This is what Earth souls are truly wanting from you. Not your words, not your preaching at them to be different, they want you YOU, yes YOU, YOU, YOU. Your presence, your being, your LIGHT that shines out of you even when you don't say a word.

Receiving the Download

And now, it is time for us to affix your interstellar communications device into your field.

Sit in your chair, with your feet flat on the floor, making sure that you are fully grounded at this process takes place. We are now beginning the installation. You may feel some tremors. This is a sign that an installation is happening into your energy field. Breathe. This might take a while in Earth time. We are installing receptors into your field that enable you to receive interstellar codes and energies. They are being affixed to your field as we speak here and as you access this paragraph. Breathe. Now good, see what you perceive that is different now. Reflect on how you are feeling and what you are noticing that has changed. What are you hearing now? Take a few moments to jot down any new insights that have come to you, or messages, or feelings, or sensations. For some of you, sensations, or changes in energy are your primary way of receiving galactic communications. Make sure to pay attention to what you get, regardless of the form that it comes in.

And congratulations, the installation is complete.

Take a few moments again to notice what is different with your way of being now. And practice connecting with your galactic guides through the new channels that have been opened up for you. You may do this simply by setting the intention to connect with them through these new receptors that are now operational in your field. The more you do this, the more these receptors strengthen and the stronger you will feel the energies and messages coming through to you. Be with these messages and do not try to censor or control what is coming through. Jot them down in their entirety diligently. They will reveal much about what is happening in the galaxy, and the roles that you are here to play in the galaxy through your Earth mission and experience.

(Note to Reader from Gil: This activation is very subtle and the changes in the frequencies operating in your energy field may manifest as very fine and subtle sensations that are detected by each individual in their own unique ways. The next section speaks of practicing using this activation to strengthen receiving interstellar communications.)

Strengthening and Using the Download

Write down the messages you receive regardless of what they are. You may get a message one day where it is a certain galactic group introducing themselves to you and telling you about them. And you may not understand what is the reason this is coming through. Let go of needing to understand and simply note the message anyway in your notepad. There are usually larger reasons for what you receive that may not always be communicated to you at the outset. And then when the time is right, another deeper message may be passed on to you that gives you the 'a-ha' around why the first message came through the way it did, that sheds the light of, 'Oh, that now makes sense to me,' on the first message you got. And keep on going, because each message tends to illuminate and build on the previous, and there are usually consistent themes that overhang across all of the messages that come through to be received by you.

Have fun playing with this! The installation is now inside of your field, and it will continue to unfold and strengthen into more places and spaces inside of you over time. You are capable of receiving communications from us. All it takes is a little faith, trust, and discipline to note what you are sensing, seeing, hearing, or otherwise perceiving as you set the intention to do so. BE the communication. BE our voice out in the world. BE the galactic being that you are, in co-creation with us. As you receive our messages and energies, the stronger you will grow in your ability to BE this on Earth.

In the next chapter, you will be receiving a different type of gift – a gift that brings you into the wisdoms, properties and deeper teachings of the water element. This is awaiting you in the next chapter, and please proceed.

Finding YourSELF for Starseeds and Lightworkers

42

Chapter 4

The Activation for the Deep Cleansing of Wounds

The Gift of the Holy Water from the Aszavariens

The Purpose of Woundings in the Human Race

We are the Aszavariens. We assist humanity in accessing their wounds and cleaning them out. Wounds are what hurts. They are often also what makes you strong and what gives you conviction to say "Yes" or "No" to something that you believe in. They tell you what can hurt, so that you can acquire the energy and the devotion to making sure it never happens again – to yourself, or to other people. They give you the firmness of being able to say, "No, you will stop bullying that child instantly," -- if you have been bullied yourself in the past. And then the courage and resolve to set up support groups for those who have been bullied. Your biggest wounds are there to point you in the direction for this lifetime that you have set for yourself before you fell into the veil of forgetfulness that comes with birth and incarnation into the 3-dimensional world.

The Purpose of Cleaning Up Your Wounds

Many people live with their wounds for a long long time, defining themselves by their wounds, accumulating the energies of anger and hatred as time passes, and living only to protect themselves from being hurt further in those same places where they have been hurt before. To you, we say, it's time to stop doing that. Stop shrinking down, stop contracting your aura, stop limiting what you do and be from a place of fear and desire to protect yourself. Open up to the vastness of the Universe by courageously rising up and taking the risk of being hurt again – yes you heard right, the risk of being hurt again. For it is the willingness to live with this risk that allows you to encounter your wounds, to come face to face with them, and to finally release all the scabs, all the old energies of hatred, pain, anger, sadness, hopelessness that you were clutching onto. Only when you take the risk to allow the wound to come exposed can it finally disinfect, reveal its message, and return you all the energy that it has been hoarding from you all this while - energy that can transform and transmute into beautiful light that shows you the way into your own path and glory. Energy that vitalizes instead of devitalizing all your systems. Energy that you can actually use to pursue and accelerate you on your true path in life.

The Gift of the Aszavariens

We give you the gift of a special water that disinfects and cleans your wounds. This water is special. It is of a lighter, cleaner vibration than waters that you may encounter on Earth. It contains crystalline properties that suck out the dirt from places in your field as it penetrates into these places. It has a structure that enables it to hold dense and grimy energies and carry them away with it. This is the Holy Water of Aszavarios, and something that we present to you at this time for your use as you ascend into finer and finer vibrations. Use this to cleanse your field of the dirt and grimes that have been dragging you down and keeping you bound by their weight against your desire to proceed with empowerment along your path. Use this to rid yourself of the fears and defenses that tell you "No, you are ours, nowhere shall you be going". These fears and defenses are the stuff of your past that is in fear of you making different choices for your life and thereby triggering the risk of opening up the old wounds that they are anxiously guarding with all their might - the risk of you stepping into places where you might end up getting hurt again in the same way as you did in the past.

Deep Cleansing and Its Processes

This water brings in a number of different energies into your field. It brings in the energy of soothing, consolation, and gradual enrollment into allowing the defenses that are protecting your wounds to drop away. It speaks to these defenses, understands the reason for their being, and holds space for their process and gradual transformation into insight and enlightenment. It brings a cleansing frequency into the places where you are holding wounds, allowing the wounds to transmute, heal, and finally form painless scabs and a new patterning on you that give you your personality, your unique-to-you traits, and a wisdom that derives from having processed through and survived these wounds. It helps you go from wounded to wise and empowered *because* of the wounding. This is the gift of the Holy Water of Aszavariens and what it does.

This water is a gift that must be used with care. It is powerful, and it comes with teachings that not every wound inside of you (and human beings have many) is ready for. For wounds can sometimes hurt so much that they are blinded to change – they actively resist and fight against change. It can seem strange. "But I am here to make you feel better!" "No, I no longer trust anyone or anything," is sometimes the response that is automatically triggered in someone who is hurting so much. For people with trust issues, using the water is not the way for their healing. People with trust issues resist and reject anything foreign or external that attempts to help them. In these instances, the only thing that can be done is to be patient, and hold space. These people need to work it out for themselves, and the water simply holds them in a protective space to cushion their process for them and have it be gentler as they re-experience their pains over and over again until they get released fully. 'Gentleness' is the operative word here. While the water cannot assist in dealing with the wound directly, it can be a cheerleader from the side, encouraging you to lower your defences and to allow what is behind these defences to gradually emerge into the light, even if this must be done repeatedly at low intensity over a period of time. It gives patience, forbearance, and stamina for this to continue and continue, even if all efforts are met with distrust and rejection repeatedly. It is the social worker who never gives up hope, repeatedly knocking on the door until the day that you are ready to unlock the door to meet it and receive its assistance.

Preparing to Receive the Gift of The Holy Water

We present this gift of water to you with our love and blessings. Let it enter all parts of your field that are ready for it. Allow it to wash away pain, hatred, anguish, anger. Release these and let the water take it away. All you need to do is be, and let these be taken away. There is nothing you need to do except to allow the water to do its job. The water cannot enter places inside of you where you are holding resistance, where you have clammed up, where you have closed yourself up and don't want to heal. It cannot enter the places where you want to do it all alone and refuse support, or the places where you think you can do it better on your own. The water will hold space in those places, and it cannot enter unless you allow it to, until you take a deep breathe and make a conscious choice to release all your tension and resistance. Yes, conscious choice. You need to know where inside of you you are resisting help, where you are not trusting energies from the outside to be of assistance, where you say, 'No thanks, I'll do this on my own', where you disbelieve that anything can truly help you.

47

Ask yourself the following:

a) Where are you hurting so much that you don't want anyone else to know about?

b) Where are you holding secrets that you fear others will find out?

c) What could make you open up about these parts of yourself? Under what circumstances might this be possible?

d) What is the real fear behind letting others know about these secrets/parts of yourself?

e) What do you believe about yourself that you fear that others will find out about?

f) Would you be willing to believe that others can be supportive rather than critical towards all this that you are hiding about yourself?

g) And finally, what could you potentially do or say to support others who are hiding similar things to encourage them and let them know that it is safe to speak about what they are hiding / do not wish to speak of?

Take a pen and some paper and write down your responses to the questions above. We are with you holding space as you reflect on the questions, encouraging you to go deeper into the places inside of you that you may be afraid of confronting, and which are therefore the places where you are closing yourself up to the healing of the water. Allow these parts of you to arise as you write. Simply allow, and hear them. That is the key to allowing them to be released, to allowing them to receive the gift of deep cleansing that we will be activating for you later in this chapter.

It is important that you take the time to respond to these questions to the best of your ability. Because for many people on Earth, it is not the incapacity to heal that is the stumbling block but rather the lack of real desire to, often from a fear for what 'can of worms' this will open up if they were to confront all that is tucked away in the storeroom. As an analogy, cleaning your system is a bit like cleaning your house. You have all this old stuff in your storeroom, inside your cupboards, in your garage, in your kitchen cabinets, and God knows what you're going to find in them once you're turning all of them out. Cockroaches, ants, lizards, all sorts of nasty creepy crawlies that you would rather leave hidden and sleeping. Some people would rather not clean so that they don't have to deal with this stuff. They would rather live with the mess inside of their house till the end of their days than take a determined broom, deodorant and bottle of insecticide to clear everything out. And the latter is what we are asking of you to do in the questions above, in order to enable you to receive the full benefits of the cleansing water that we are preparing to download into your system in short course.

It is time for you to make a choice now to say, "Yes, I am willing to clean house. This process may not feel comfortable. I may not like what I find inside of myself. And there it is, it is going to get cleaned out. NOW." Believe us, it will get easier as you go through the process. It starts becoming easier because each time you clean house, you get better and more efficient at cleaning the next time. And at some point, this will become second nature to you – to take a broom to all the dirt that accumulates in your system periodically. You get good at maintenance and you actually come to enjoy it. Because the cleaner you are, the better you feel, the more light can come into your system to fill you up with new insights, new stirrings, new inspirations for things to do on the Earth that align with your mission. The more space you have, the more we can fill you up with great product ideas, downloads, and energies that you can pass on to others. And this is why we are inviting you at this time to clean up. And for sure, you can.

Receiving the Activation – The Process

These are the steps for receiving the activation, which we are presenting to you now as you read the text in this paragraph.

1. Make sure that you are fully prepared, that you have made your responses to all of the preparatory questions above to the best of your ability.

2. We are handing you the gift of holy water right now. Feel it. Allow it to permeate your entire energy field.

3. Notice how it is going into places and space where you are holding tension, pain, and other constrictions, that you may not even have noticed. See, hear, feel or know the dirt coming out from these places and spaces – old dense energies. See, hear, feel or know the gift of water entering into even deeper places and spaces in you.

4. Notice where you may be rejecting the gift. Allow yourself to release the rejection by saying to the water, "I welcome you." Allow the water to continue running through your system. Allow the water to bless all those parts of you that are in pain. Allow the water to wash away your wounds.

5. There are some parts of you that may contract as the water enters. Take a deep breath, and allow them to release. Know that it will be okay. This is a blessing that is coming to you. Allow the water to do its job. It make take a few minutes before you are thoroughly permeated by the water. Simply be, and allow, during this time.

6. You may find yourself coughing, or spurting, or clearing your nose, or releasing old energies in other ways, shapes or forms. This IS the water doing its job.

When the process is complete, you will typically get a sense that it is done. It is a strong activation. So be gentle on yourself, and allow yourself to take a break to integrate. You may feel like taking a walk outside, or just doing nothing for a while so that you can be with yourself, or doing something entirely different than what you were doing before the activation entered into your system. Follow these instincts, as this is part of your integration of the activation. You will typically feel something different after the activation is complete. New directions arising, new thoughts arising, new feelings arising, that tell you to be and do differently. Notice what these are, and write them down to anchor in the new energies that you have received and to become aware of the new lights that have entered you. It is always important to notice what has changed so that it can come into your awareness, take root, and grow bigger as time goes by.

Anchoring in the Activation onto the Physical Plane

Together with this activation comes a blessing from us. This is a blessing for your highest awareness of how your wounds have determined the way that you have lived – who you have become and what you have done as a result of them. For as you become aware of them, not only can you see how they have controlled your life hitherto, but also understand the purposes that they have played in your life, and the bigger message that they have been wanting to give to you. Because all wounds are really energies that are pushing you towards the path that is most appropriate for your soul's direction and mission. Once you can appreciate what the wound has done for your path, it is no longer necessary for you to encounter it again and again and again. You can now be free from its message since you have heard it, integrated it, and used its energies to illuminate a roadmap towards your highest destinies for your life. The wound is the dangerous beast that a journeyer encounters on their path that tells the journeyer where they are supposed to go by barking at the journeyer where NOT to go.

So look at all the places where you are in pain and ask them:

a)   What are you telling me NOT to do, or where are you blocking me from going? What is the warning that you are issuing me?

b)   Where really, are you then pointing me towards?

c)   What makes me want to hold on to you? What am I really in fear of encountering if I heed your warning and change course?

d)   What will you do to me if I persist in heading down the same direction that has caused me to crash headlong into you? How will you break me eventually if I persist in continuing the same course that has taken me towards you?

e)   Where can I begin to allow myself to change my course so that I can finally start moving towards the path that is truly mine?

f)   What messages of support are there really embedded and overhanging in this experience that are encouraging me to move onto my real path if I make the choice to view the situation as a positive signal for change?

g)   Where can I make the changes that the lessons of this (or these types of) experience have taught me?

h)   What types of changes can I make?

These reflections will enable you to get the most out of each activation that you receive for the Holy Water, bringing awareness to the real messages being communicated by the pains, wounds, and hurts that are still existing in your energy field and body. It is crucial that you listen to their messages, for they will continue trying to get your attention in the only way that they can (i.e. by stinging you really badly) for as long as you ignore them, for as long as you refuse to pay heed to their warnings. The activation for the Holy Water will assist these wounds and pains in being brought to light – it will assist you in *getting* their messages much more clearly and easily so that you can finally listen and take action to make the changes that they have been advocating that you make since they started sending pain signals to you. It is up to you to accept their message, to acknowledge the important point(s) they are making to you, and to decide how to integrate into your life the changes that they are asking for you to make in a manner that is sustainable, workable, and honours the message that they are bringing you.

As you do this, the old pains and hurts will cease to hurt as much. And slowly, little by little, they will start to dissipate and disappear as time goes by and the changes they are advocating are built more and more into your life until they become second nature to you. The energies that are causing you pain leave when you have integrated fully their messages and warnings into the entire structure for your life. Meaning that, they leave when you are planning and designing your life giving due account to what they are attempting to tell you and they are satisfied that they have been heard. They leave when they are satisfied that you are taking their messages and warnings very seriously and consciously when you make choices for how you treat yourself, how you plan your day, what you will do and what you will not do, and what you will invest your energy into and what you will not invest your energy into. They leave when you have received and honored all of their wisdoms.

Remember that when there is a pain, it is a signal for a change.

Going Onward

We leave you now in this chapter with this. In the next chapter, you will be taking a journey to encounter yourself, particularly all those parts of yourself that you feel reviled by, that you fear, that you don't wish to accept, and you will be working with all these parts of yourself to retrieve their light and wisdom and special energies.

The Pleisatarians are awaiting you in the next chapter to guide you on this stage of your journey that is coming next.

Chapter 5

The Activation for the EnJoyment of True Self

The Gift of the Box of True You from the Pleisatarians[2]

---

[2] *Note to Readers from Gil: Pleisatarians is pronounced 'Please-ahhh-tarians'.*

Your Relationship with Yourself

Greetings our friend! We come before you, as the Pleisatarians. We come to you to invite you to examine your relationship with yourself. How do you feel about yourself? Do you feel irritated and irked at yourself? Do you feel that nothing about you is good enough? Yes, you might say. I feel as if I can't love myself. I look at myself and feel that it is insufficient in some way. I feel as if some part of me isn't living up to the standards that I want it to live up to. I want myself to be better. I want all these things about myself to be better.

Why do you grasp so much at your faults? We ask you. Look at what you are doing every single day, dismissing yourself that this about you is no good, that everything about yourself is flawed, telling yourself that it is not enough, that nothing about you is enough. You do this because you want to improve, yes. And we understand that you want to improve, you want to do better, because it all seems to hang on you getting better at everything so that everything around you can get better. It feels as if everything hinges on you, and you are therefore the critical linchpin that CANNOT be a failure in any single way. You must be great at every single thing, you must make sure everything about you meets your required standards. And nothing about you is at all sufficient where it is now.

The Universe Loves You

Relax! We tell you. Relax…Take a deep breath. We understand your desire to make everything go better, to make yourself do better, to have yourself go faster. And we tell you, breathe… Look around you. The Universe is smiling at you. The Universe loves you. The Universe loves you exactly the way you are. Yes, as you are right now. We need you exactly the way you are right now, replete with all of the things you feel are your faults and insufficiencies.

But how can this be? There are so many things about me that need to be improved. This thing that I am not good at. That other thing that I really am not good at. All these things about me that need some fixing. How am I useful or competent for any mission at all the way that I am? No, no, no, let me get round to fixing all these things about myself. Let me deal with all these things first about myself before we talk about anyone loving me. Let me fix this stuff first, alright? Hold the loving me part first, and let me get round to fixing all these different things about me that really really need to be improved as soon as possible - aka yesterday.

To this, we hold a space of laugher and compassion. For in your infinite wisdom, the one thing that you have missed is to stop your fixing, and simply BE and enjoy yourself. Yes, to BE. To stop and simply BE. BE, BE, BE. Yes, to BE. You've got it now. To BE. In this moment, where all is silent, and what is present is yourSelf, and something new awakens. Feel it?

The Strengths that are YOU

Hmm. You may feel. This is new. BE-ing, that has nothing to do with DO-ing. Yes, we say. Feel the silence of BE-ing. In this moment, where there is only you, as you are. Where you are simply as you are. Where you are part of the Universe, a constituent part of the Universe, part of a grander whole, part of a tapestry that is unique in itself, with every single thing about you making YOU the uniqueness that you are. This tapestry has many different colours, and each person is a unique colour, with everything about that person making them the unique colour that they are.

What is unique about me then? You may ask, now curious and inquisitive. What colours and textures and nuances do I contribute to this tapestry of the Universe? Where is my unique value here, that is me?

Ah, that is the real question, isn't it? Where are you NOT seeing the unique colours and nuances that you really are that are resplendently contributing to the weave of the world? Where can you begin to see this more? Where can you start appreciating the colours and music and textures that you are bringing through to the world through your presence – through you being YOU?

And this is where you bring out your pen and paper and we embark on a wonderful reflection exercise to discover the colours that you contribute to the fabric of this world.

Reflect on this…

a) Where are your strengths? What are you really good at? What is really wonderful about you that you often take for granted in your desire to focus on the things that you think you are weak at?

b) What are these strengths telling you about where you can contribute very strongly in the world?

c) What do these strengths tell you about you?

And stay focused on your strengths... yes we know the weaknesses are more compelling to you, and do come back and stay focused here on the STRENGTHS. Great. Now that we have your attention back again, let's continue.

d) What can you do MORE of with your strengths? Where do your strengths really want to be expressed out in the world?

e) Where do you see yourself being able to contribute more at using the strengths that you have?

Pause for a moment and reflect on these questions. Allow yourself to take them in fully. This could feel uncomfortable, yes. Strengths? Oopf, you might say. I've never really focused much on them. Do I really have them? Perhaps I do, okay. Let me see how I can work with them. Let me use them more often. Let me get to know them better. That I supposed I can do. Yes, okay.

And breathe, we say. STRENGTHS. Yes, you DO have them. Big and strong ones too, that are waiting for you to acknowledge them, so that they may emerge and play a pivotal role in your life. So that they may point you towards a direction for growth that is uniquely yours to take. So that they can guide you on a path that is the easiest for you as you navigate what may sometimes seem like the thicket of life here on the planet. Your strengths point you towards your true path. They give you the greatest hints of where even bigger gifts might be lying waiting for you as you walk your path.

Appreciate your strengths. Your strengths are a lot of what make you You.

The Gift of the Pleisatarians

And now, we would like to present you with the gift of the Box of True You. This is a special box. It contains two energies mixed together. The first is the energy of lavender-purple light, which reveals to you your strengths, especially those that you have consistently denied to yourself – those at which you have consistently said, 'No, no, no, no, no, that's not me,' when they are pointed out at you, when they are presented at you. Lavender brings in an energy of persistence that tells you, 'But yes, it really is you, THAT'. And the energy of lavender stays until you cannot but take a look at what it is telling you and start appreciating that there really might be something in there for you. Lavender is the friend who is gentle yet persistent in its presence - so much so that that their message slowly percolates into your consciousness as time goes by, even if it takes a slow while. Lavender gets you to accept your strengths and all that is you, AND to see every single thing about you as a strength. It tells you how every single thing that you believe is a flaw IS a strength, for these give you the energies to grow and to blossom into something even more beautiful that is already emerging. Where you are focused on finding fault about yourself in the present, Lavender is the voice that tells you to look to the future, at what is arriving out of your present conditions that can come ONLY because of your present conditions. It brings in appreciation of who you are at the present moment that is the seed for the flower that is arriving – and who you are who is therefore the flower that is already embedded in the present. Lavender represents the blossom that is already inscribed inside your DNA base coding, that has been set to emerge in Divine Timing.

Connecting to Yourself

The Box of True You also contains the energies of yellow-white light. This energy represents purity and clarity. It represents the purity of being the way you are exactly as you are, without the taint of judgments, criticisms, or fault-finding FROM yourself (primarily!). It represents the clarity of seeing yourself exactly as you are, no holds barred. Because truly, there is nothing to fear about seeing yourself exactly as who you are. You are you. You are sacred. You are pure as you are in this moment now, when it is simply you, and all else is silent.

White is also the colour of connection. In this case, it assists you in connecting with yourself, in knowing all aspects of yourself, including the ones that you don't want to see, the ones that you would rather keep buried, the parts of you that you have rejected. The energy of white light tells you, 'Hey, stay with me please. Be with me. Simply be with me, period'. It is an invitation to BE, period, end of story. It is an invitation to stay silent, to stay in NOW time, and be with yourself. It tells you to stay, when you would rather run and hide, or run and do something else, or run and try to fix yourself. It silences your mental conversations that take you away from being, so that the only choice left open for you on the table is to BE. The energy of white brings you back towards yourself. It enfolds you into yourself.

Clarity at Who You Are

As white light mixes with yellow light, it brings forth a unique mixture of energies that tell you, 'Be with yourself and see clearly who you are!' 'Do not be afraid of being with yourself. Yes, see

63

yourself clearly'. It illuminates who you are for you to see. It helps you release judgment and fear around what you may see there. It brings you straight into the bullseye of all that you are, cutting through the fog of denials, disbeliefs, and preconceptions that you already have about what you are going to find there. It ignores all falsehoods and goes straight to the point.

And this is the gift from us, the Pleisatarians. This is the gift and blessing that we give to you, that you may come to see yourself clearly and enjoy yourself dearly, that you may revel in all of your strengths - which includes and which means ALL of you.

Receiving the Activation

And now, it is time for you to receive this gift.

1. Take a deep breath first, for this is a strong download. When you are ready let us know.

2. When you give us the signal by indicating YES, we will push the energies of the Box of True You into your crown chakra and third eye, from where the activation will occur. Are you ready? Say yes if you are.

3. And, we have pushed the download into your field now. Breathe. Allow the energies to permeate through your entire body. Feel, hear, or see them percolate through your entire field.

4. You may find places in your body that are resisting the energy – allow these to relax and welcome the changes that are occurring.

5. Breathe. BE, simply BE in silence as the energy integrates into your field and takes you into the silence of Being. And stay there, for as long as is appropriate, until you feel this state of BEing integrate into you. Until the silence becomes a part of your Being that is inseparable from you.

How do you feel now? Take the time to notice what is different now. Take the time to sense, to Be. Breathe. What are you hearing now that you didn't hear before? What are you feeling now that you didn't feel before? What do you know now that you didn't know before? What is it that has changed? Take some time to be with yourself in all these changes.

Anchoring in the Activation into Your Energy Field

And then when you are ready, please take a pen and some paper, and write down what you experienced here in this activation. This helps you anchor in the changes into your field and open the pathways for the activation to occur even more deeply and strongly should you decide to re-read this chapter again and receive it a second time. The energy of silence is now anchoring even more deeply into your field. In this silence, you simply are. There is no mind chatter about where you need to fix yourself, about the thousand things you need to do to make things better about you, there is no looking back in self-blame and regret of where you ought to have done better at points in your past. Be in this silence. Observe the joy emerge in this silence. Feel the joy of being YOU. Be in this joy of being you. En-Joy yourself. En-Joy You.

Congratulations! You have received the activation for the Enjoyment of True You.

The Next Gift

In the next chapter, another related gift awaits you, from the Escortarians. The Escortarians bring teachings and wisdoms on dealing with the places where you are judging yourself the most, where you are holding on to the deepest pains, and they teach you gently how to release these internal knots.

Please turn the page and proceed to the next stage of your journey.

Chapter 6

The Activation for Self-Compassion

The Gift of The Golden Fire for the Heart from the Escortarians

Welcome! Welcome to the internal world of where you are hurting the most inside of you. We are the Escortarians, and we bring you into this world as your guides and teachers. Our task here is not to try to heal you. No, that is not our purpose. Our task is to help you be and come face to face with your pain. What? What is the point of this? You may ask. Why do you bring me to my pain, and then expect me to do nothing about it except stare at it and be with it? Why can't we do anything about it? Why can't we do something about it? What is the point of this entire exercise if not to get something done with this pain that is sticking out like a sore thumb?

Compassion as a State of Being with – Not Fixing – Pain

To this we say, let your pain speak. Deny it not, try to fix it not, and instead, let it speak to you about what is hurting, and what it desperately needs from you. Yes, listen to it. Hear its screams. Hear its complaints. Listen to it tell you about every single thing that it wants and needs from you that you have been denying it.

What does that even mean? You may ask. Listen to it? I can't hear it. I see only what I need to do, what I need to push for in order to move forward. I see only the path ahead. And this pain of which you speak, it drags me back. It stops me from going where I want to go, from being where I need to be. It needs to GO. I need it to get away from me right NOW.

To that we say, it won't go away, until you are fully able to be with it, hear it, empathize with it, and respect the needs that it is expressing to you. It will not go away until it is fully seen, and heard, and understood. It will continue tearing at you until you have made space and time for its message of pain. It cannot fully be laid to peace and rest until such time as the world can slow down at long last and pay attention to what it has to say instead of trying to reduce it, fix it, and make it go away or diminish somewhat. That means YOU slowing down and allowing it to be it, regardless of what you may think of it, or how you prefer it to be, or what you believe it needs to shift into going into the future.

All pain is a distress sign for something that is not going well inside of your system. It is a signal for something that needs attention right here right now. A signal for you to STOP and LOOK HERE. A demand for you to take the time to be with what is calling out for you to listen. When you have pain that won't go away, it is a call for you to open your heart and be with it, and to do nothing except that.

When you open your heart at something that is hurting, when you open your heart at pain, when you do nothing except be that heart-full presence in the encountering of all that lies inside you that is in pain, this is compassion.

Yes, feel your heart opening now. Feel its petals blossom. Inside of your heart lies petals upon petals, layers upon layers of petals. Feel them bloom one by one. As they bloom, your pain starts to look different. Instead of being a nuisance, the parts of you that are in pain become instead precious pieces of you that are there to be nurtured, that are for you to be with in a space of empathy and understanding as the energy of your heart envelops them and holds them in its field. And through that holding of space for them with your heart, these pieces of you have the opportunity to transform into something different. Something more awakened.

Something more self-realized. Something with greater insight and illumination. A transformation of these pain pieces takes place.

This is a practice. It is a practice to open your heart each time you encounter something uncomfortable, something that you would rather not be there, something that you can't wait to get rid of as soon as possible if you had the choice. Such irritants are energies that are wanting your attention. Give them the attention of your heart and see what happens. Watch them transform. Watch them dissolve and transform as the energies and field of your heart melt away their edges, their complaints, their discontent, and their pain. Watch the knots that are hurting inside of you come untied. Watch them stretch open, release their tension, and unwind to receive the light into places that were previously knotted up. Watch them unfold and realize something radically different about the nature of the problem that they were previously all knotted up in, that they could not see a solution to.

The Nature of Knots or 'Nots'

Many pains or distress occur because of knots. Or rather, they have the energetic structure of knots. They look all wound up, tied up, the energy does not move. Things are clenched up, and the same problem is encountered again and again. It feels frustrating because no matter how you move, it always feels as if you're back to the same point, that nothing can untie this energy and make it flow. It's all hemmed up and it stays in the same place all the time, refusing to move despite all your attempts to have it change into something different. It can manifest as a tension in your body. A pain in your body at the same spot that won't go away. Or a particular difficult person in your life that won't budge. Or a situation where everyone isn't budging, and you are all wound up and irritated as a result. The energy isn't flowing despite all your attempts, and you are at a point of serious frustration as a result.

A knot is a signal that tells you – open your heart. Open your heart and see what happens! Where people are telling you NO, opening your heart allows them to say YES. When people are telling you that things can-'kNOT' be done, open your heart to allow new light to come in to illuminate the truths of the problem and the hidden pathways where things CAN get done and resolved. Your heart stretches open energies that were previously knotted up, where things were tied up in kNOTs. It allow knotted energies to unfold more easily and flow towards the possibilities for resolution that are already there in plain sight. Knots come untied when the heart stretches to stretch them apart. And this is one of the functions of the heart – to open up the space for new light to come in to what was previously all knotted up. The heart has the capacity to stretch everyone in a challenging situation beyond their previous limits and to enhance everyone's capacity to receive and hold more light.

Transmuting kNOTs into CANs

The heart is a special field within the human body. A strong heart field generates electromagnetic effects that touch and can be felt by all that come into the field. This field stretches and expands patterns of being wound up that people who come into contact with it are running in their energy fields. Where people are focused on their kNOTs, a strong heart field encourages them to expand and stretch their kNOTs into CANs, and expands their possibilities. The heart tells a pattern that has knotted up all its possibilities to 'Stop, and go this other way', where 'this other way' is something outside of the pattern's existing ideas of what is possible and what is not. The pattern then unravels in a totally unexpected direction, and the kNOT unwinds itself, releasing a new vitality to what previously looked like an impossible situation that enables it now to flow better towards a healthy resolution.

When you are faced with something painful, something that won't go away despite how much you try, reflect upon the following:

a) Where have you limited your possibilities in this? What do you believe you CAN'T do, that you persist in believing in so much?

b) What is causing your 'NOTs' in this situation?

c) What CAN you actually do, if you allow yourself that possibility?

d) What is your full range of 'CANs', if you were to wipe everything away and start from a total clean slate? If you started right from scratch, what different types of things would you be wanting to do here that you can quite probably figure out a way to do?

Take a pen and some paper, and spend some time reflecting on the questions above. Allow yourself to think out of the box with these questions. Where you find yourself tying yourself up in a 'kNOT', switch to letting your heart take over and answering instead from the space of your heart. Listen to what your heart says that is different from the 'kNOT' you have been insisting upon yourself. Be surprised at the wisdom of your heart. Allow all of the responses of your heart to be recorded on your paper, resisting the censorship of your mind that you are so accustomed to applying to the natural flow of words from your heart.

When you have finished this exercise, pick up your paper and read through all your responses one by one, especially those that have been provided to you through your heart. Notice any patterns in these responses that are indicating something deeper that your heart is wanting to communicate to you, or has been wanting to communicate to you for some time now. Be with your heart as you go through the responses. Allow yourself to use these responses to connect even more deeply into your heart, into layers that are even deeper than those that you are already naturally tapped into.

As you do this exercise, your heart is speaking to you. BE with these messages from your heart, and apply them as best as you can in your life. Ask yourself the following questions:

a) Where can I follow-through with what my heart is consistently telling me through these messages?

b) Where in my life is my heart counselling a change?

c) Where do I need to be easier, more patient, and more compassionate with myself?

d) What can I do to give myself more space and more time in these places in my life that my heart is flagging out to me?

As these insights come into your realization, they are anchored more and more into your energy field. Be with these insights, and cherish them. Note them down on your piece of paper and make it a point to implement them in your life. These are signals from a wise part of you that is providing you with some deep advice for changes to make in your life that will assist you in more fully stepping into the energy of compassion for yourself. They point the way towards you being able to open the fullness of your heart to yourself.

The Gift of the Escortarians

The gift that we have for you here at this stage of your journey through the book is a Ball of Golden Fire that contains the energies of Divine Compassion. We place this in your heart, where it will assist your heart in generating the natural energies of compassion that each and every person already has inside of themselves. The ball also stretches and expands your heart in multiple directions, so that it can encompass more and remain open more of the time. We give this to you that you may have more compassion for yourself and – by the same token – more compassion for others.

This gift installs inside of your heart and expands over time using the energies of your own heart to fuel it. It collects your heart energies and uses it to expand, and to permeate more and deeper layers of your heart until it has transmuted all the walls that are keeping the petals of your heart closed. It works bit by bit to open each petal inside all of the chambers of your heart chakra.

Instructions for Receiving the Activation

Now, we are ready to give you this activation.

1. Prepare yourself by sitting comfortably in a chair. Know that this activation is going to enter straight into your heart chakra.

2. When you are ready, simply ask to receive the activation. You may invite the activation with a simple phrase like, "I am ready for it."

3. Feel, see, hear or know the golden ball coming into the center of your heart chakra. Feel, see, hear or know it growing and glowing brighter and brighter inside of your heart.

4. You may hear the fiery-golden energies speak to you, blazing inside you. Breathe. Allow it to permeate your entire heart chakra. Breathe again as it makes its way into the different chambers of your heart.

5. Notice where the energies of the activation are encountering resistance inside of your heart, which may manifest as a sensation of pain in certain segments of your heart. Breathe, and set the intention to allow these walls to melt into the golden-fiery ball of energies. Breathe deeply, and with each out breath, release all these resistances.

6. You will see, hear, feel or know the ball of energy percolating even more deeply into chambers that you did not even realize existed. Breathe again as this happens. Feel the petals of your heart opening up and releasing their energies, enriching your heart chakra as a whole.

7. See, hear, feel or know your heart chakra blossoming like a flower. Feel the sense of peace that naturally occurs as your heart opens. Stay in this peaceful place for a moment – or many more moments, as you wish.

8. Notice now what has changed in the way that you feel towards one or two things that you previously found irritating or distasteful in your life. How are you feeling now towards them? How does your heart feel towards them? Where can you now be more compassionate towards them?

And congratulations! You have now received the activation for self-compassion.

Anchoring in the Activation Strongly

You may choose to anchor the activation even more strongly into your field by reflecting on where in your life you have been beating yourself up instead of letting your heart have a more powerful voice in the way that you think and feel about yourself. Reflect on the following:

a) What are you harsh and uncompromising to yourself about?

b) What does your heart truly say about this now?

c) Where do you resist the messages of compassion for yourself that your heart is attempting to bring to you?

d) What reasons do you give for refusing this compassion?

e) What would your heart – from its deepest bottom – say in response to these reasons that you give for not being compassionate with yourself?

f) Where might you be willing to give your heart more space to be the decider of how you think, feel and treat yourself in life?

g) What action will you take to follow-through in these areas of your life where you are willing to let your heart be the decider for how you are going to treat yourself?

Self-Compassion NOW!

Pat yourself now on your back for having gone through this process, and diligently reflecting on these questions. Yes, there is always still work to do, there is always going to be more that is waiting to rise up to your conscious awareness vis-à-vis the questions above. And at this time, it is equally important to be in your heart space NOW and allow your heart to tell you what a wonderful job you've already done here, and to thank you for bringing yourself on this journey into Finding YourSelf. Put aside all the distracting thoughts going on in your head telling you that the work is not complete, that there is a lot more to go, that there is a lot more to do before things get to the place where you can be fully satisfied at them – and at yourself. Take this moment to do nothing except sit in your heart. And from the space of your heart, allow yourself to look out with compassion at the entire world, and at yourself. All is as it is right now, and All will be as it will be, All of this. From the space of your heart, All simply IS.

Juicy Closures

What have you learnt from this chapter? We would love to hear from you on this. How does your heart feel about it all?

In the next chapter, you will be receiving something different – a gift that expands your consciousness in multiple realms. Please proceed forward.

Chapter 7

The Activation for Awakening to Your Multi-Dimensional Presence

The Gift of Multi-Dimensional Consciousness from the Aesquarians

The Nature of Multi-Dimensional Consciousness

Wе are the Aesquarians. Our gift to you is one that may bring forth the energy of surprise into your life – a surprise awakening into something that you never saw before, that you have never encountered before. An awakening into a bigger reality that is simply breathtaking. For we are here to bring you into realms that you never realized before were there. Realms that were always there, yes, present in your field, that you yet never paid attention to in your habitual focus on the 3-dimensional world. These are realms that have existed since the beginning of time. Realms where a lot of activity takes place, including much of what is going on in terms of the support that is being moved to all the starseeds on Earth. These are realms in which we galactic beings operate, where we are actively coordinating packages of downloads and energies to support the physical plane. Realms that you access when you actively open a channel to us to receive our presence and downloads. Realms that you will increasingly awaken to and be able to become fully conscious of as your level of spiritual mastery grows and your blocks to seeing us, feeling us, hearing us, and accessing us fall apart one by one.

Accessing Multi-Dimensional Realms

We call you to these realms now. Hear us speak. Hear us! As you read through this text, we are assisting you in opening your channels to the realms that we inhabit, and beyond.

For millions of years, human beings have not been conscious of the multi-dimensional realms, of the multitude of things that are taking place in the galaxy. Most of this has been invisible as human beings had their eyes and ears closed to anything beyond the 3-dimensional world in a stubborn refusal to see and understand that there was anything more. "No, I can only see here and now, I can only see what is before me, and this is it," they believe. "There is nothing else, so don't try to convince me that there is anything else. There is only what I can see before me. What I can feel, and touch, and smell, and hear, in this 3-dimensional box of mine. There is nothing else beyond this box." And they stubbornly cling on to the walls of the box despite all our attempts to appear within the box in various shapes, ways and forms to awaken them to a much larger reality that lies outside, to tell them, 'Hey, look at the realities outside of this box!' They stubbornly cling on to the walls to preserve their sense of control over the single only reality that they can perceive. Because what lies beyond is astounding, and WILL challenge every single one of their ideas and beliefs on the size and scope and functions of the Universe, of Earth's function, place and purpose in the Universe, AND of their own role, place and purpose on Earth given Earth's place in the cosmos. In this grander scheme of things, all that they were taught to believe about themselves starts to break down. Many people would rather be blind to this larger reality than embrace the grandeur of the true nature of things, which leads to all sorts of uncomfortable questions about the nature of self, and the nature of one's self in the Universe. For the awakening to this larger reality will inevitably lead to a breaking down of the ego self that tries so desperately to cling on to its existing identity for fear of losing its individuated consciousness against the tide of underlying oneness that is the true reality of all in the Universe.

The Starseed Consciousness

As a starseed, you already know all of this. Innately, intuitively, you already know of all that is taking place in the galaxy. You may not know the full details, or this may not be in your conscious awareness every single moment of your life on the 3-dimensional plane, and you may not even be always aware of when we are trying to communicate with you. Or, you may even be actively resisting our communications with you out of a misplaced belief that they will hinder rather than assist you. Yet, on some deeper level, you have always known of something much larger than yourself. Yes, on a deeper level, you do know of us. You have always known that there is *something* – even if you cannot quite put your finger on it. And this *something* drives you at a very core level, at a very deep and fundamental level of your being. It gives your entire life structure, and meaning, and direction, even if you may not be fully conscious of what, or where, or how, and even if parts of you try to resist it. Even when your mind questions what is going on, your soul continues to drive your life, bringing you in the direction that you have already decided to take for this lifetime before you came into incarnation. For your soul has absolutely no doubts over where you are headed in this lifetime.

This is the nature of multi-dimensional consciousness. It is the feeling, the inkling, that hits you out of nowhere, that you yet cannot shake off and demands to be taken seriously. It is the inner knowing that you have, the knowing that has no doubts. It is the direction that you seem to take instinctively, even if you don't fully understand why, or didn't even realize you took until you have the benefit of hindsight. It is the big booming voice that you see, hear, know, or feel that seems to come from the outside to convey a strong message or suggestion about what you ought to be doing or being as a next step.

All of these are different forms of multi-dimensional activities, signals, and consciousnesses. And when you engage with these, you are participating in the multi-dimensional realms. When you hear a message and when you allow it to sink into your field. When you sense the presence of angels above you. When you feel guided and supported by presences around you. Many beings of the multi-dimensional realms surround each and every single one of you – personally. Consciously or unconsciously, you are communicating with them, and you are participating on the multi-dimensional realms. You attend meetings with them and receive messages from them in your dreams. You start having inspirations that you then act on on the physical plane. Every single waking and un-waking moment of your life, everything that takes place on the multi-dimensional realms percolates to what you get inspired to do on the physical plane. Whether you realize it or not, you are already participating.

We (i.e. all of the beings who operate on the multi-dimensional realms) have all been surrounding you for centuries. We have always been with you. We have whispered in your ears. We have provided you with advice as you navigate your choices in life. We have been with you in your distress, in your confusion, in your decisions. We have always helped you find your way through the thicket of life into your personal empowerment. We have been there, egging you on when you are wanting to bury your head in the sand and avoid moving forward. We have helped propel you forward in times when you feel too tired to go on, in times when you are on the verge of giving up. We are with you as you grow stronger and stronger, day by day, and greater and greater in consciousness. And on some level, on the deepest level of your being, you already know and appreciate this fully.

The Activation for Multi-Dimensional Consciousness

We bring you here an activation to awaken you to your multi-dimensional consciousness. This activation will assist you in becoming aware of what is going on beyond the 3-dimensional Earth plane. It will awaken you to some of the larger realities that are taking place, including those that involve starseed missions and the support that is arriving to all of you starseeds on the planet. It will enable you to be better aware of us – the star races, of what we are doing to support Earth, and of how the different groups of star races are helping different types of starseeds on the planet. It will boost your receptors to what we are doing that serves you to be aware of.

The activation does a number of things. First, it enhances your third eye senses. It opens your third eye. It enhances the clarity of your third eye. It enables your third eye to pierce through more density to capture more of the underlying realities behind what is veiled. It enables your third eye to see more, and be aware of more. It is a strong power-up of your third eye.

The activation also increases the sensitivity of your energy field to the presence of other energy fields that are surrounding you. When someone comes into your field, it allows your energy field to feel them much better, to detect what kind of energy they are bringing into your field. It allows you to become aware through your feeling sense of the people and things that are taking place in your environment.

Lastly, the activation strengthens your gut, the physical sensation that you 'get' in your third chakra region. It heightens the receptivity of your gut to signals from the multi-dimensional realms, enabling your gut to sound a strong alert if there is something that is coming in for you to pay attention to. It enables your gut to give you accurate signals to guide your actions. It enables your gut to give you that punch when it is strongly needed in order for you to do what is appropriate in a given moment.

The activation strengthens all of these multi-dimensional senses that you have. It powers them up so that you can be aware of more, and respond more appropriately to that which is taking place in the Universe in its greater totality.

Receiving the Activation

The activation is being channeled to you right now, as you read this line. Stay here for a few moments. You may hear a buzzing, or get a feeling of a buzzing taking place inside of your energy field. We are opening up more and more of your psychic channels, starting with your third eye, then your entire field, and then down to your gut. You may start to feel a sensation in your gut now, or hear something in your gut, or even hear your gut speak to you. Take a deep breath and allow the activation to continue. You may start to see, hear, feel or know the energy of the activation penetrating even more deeply into the relevant chakras, and activating the corresponding energy centers. The activation will continue taking place for a while, making its way deeper and deeper into the chakras. Allow this to happen and continue. Breathe. And, you will sense when the activation is done and when it is appropriate for you to move on.

Congratulations! You have received the activation for the awakening to your multi-dimensional consciousness. Well done!

Noticing the Changes

How did that feel? What are you noticing now? What are you sensing now? What are you 'getting' in your gut now? What are you feeling in your energy field now? Take some time to notice all of these sensations. Please take some time, if you are able to, to journal some of these down using a pen and some paper. As you write, notice also how the speed and flow of your writing has changed. Allow yourself to feel the difference. Allow yourself to notice what is flowing through you, and through your open channel(s). Notice the differences.

Take a few moments now to breathe and to be with yourself. If you can, go out into the open fields and take some time to listen to new inspirations that are coming into your field. Be by yourself. Sense the new things that are stirring inside of you. Listen to what your gut is trying to tell you – for any messages that it is passing on to you. Allow yourself to sense and pick up with your personal energy field the energies that are in your environment. Be fully present to all the multi-dimensional signals and energies that are taking place in and around you.

We are so excited for what you are going to experience and encounter on the multi-dimensional realms from this point forth and into your future. Many things await you. Many things await your discovery. Make use of all the senses that you have. Use them to pick up what is going on in the multi-dimensional realms. We await an even stronger connection with You as you awaken more and more multi-dimensionally.

Moving Onward

In the next part of your journey, you will be receiving a different type of gift – a gift of encountering and recognizing your own dazzling light. This is a gift that could take you into some uncomfortable places. So please gear up, and when you are ready, you may turn the page and proceed to the next chapter.

Chapter 8

The Activation for Realizing Your Own Light

The Gift of the Self-Mirror from the Oo-oahnaeriens[3]

---

[3] *Note to Readers from Gil: Oo-oahnaeriens is pronounced 'Ooh-woah-ahh-naerians'.*

ood day! We are the Oo-oahnaeriens. We come from a star system that is 22 trillion light years away from your solar system. We come here to offer you a gift of light.

Lights on Earth

For many hundreds of thousands of years, Earth has been in a state of energetic flux. You have had periods of glorious civilization where the light shined brightly, and human beings were enlightened. In these periods, science, rationality, literature, and kindness flourished. People treated one another respectfully and honored each being as sacred. People saw in each being more than what was on the 3-dimensional surface, seeing the subtle light and energy fields and Divinehood of each individual. People could touch and feel connected to one another. Civilization flourished under such immense light, and there were so many beings that were bright sparks of light on the planet, each a torch and flame that burned brightly in their light. Every individual lit up the planet with their gifts, with their flaming insight, with their forthrightness of truth, each blazing unique trails with their vibrant personality for all to see and appreciate.

It is now time for this light to return to Earth. After so many thousands of years, it is now time for this light to anchor into the Earth grid and light up the whole of the Earth again. Earth is due to be lit up again with powerful light.

You and Your Role in Lighting Earth Up

You play a significant part in this. You, yes, YOU. You are part of the immense amount of light that is being anchored on Earth in this special time. You are one of the many sparks that are coming to Earth at this time. You undertook to come to Earth for exactly this. Yes, you did. And you know your mission to be a light on the planet. You have never truly forgotten. So rise up and reclaim this now. Rise up, and OWN your LIGHT.

Owning Your Own Light

But what does it mean to own my own light? You ask. I don't understand this concept of my 'own light'. I can't see my own light. How do I even know that this is mine? Is it really mine? What is my light?

We tell you – look closer to see it. Look and see your own light. Where is your light? It is in what you believe in. It is in the truth that you stand for. It is in what you will not compromise on. It is in who you are that makes you YOU. Your light is your person and your BEing – in who you are as a Being. It is in what you radiate out to the world when you stand fearless of anything that tells you No to yourself.

So how do you be your light? How do you be your light and own it fully? Ask yourself the following:

a)   What do I love the most about myself? What do I really really enjoy about myself?

b)   What makes me extremely happy to do and/or be?

c)   What kind of circumstances make me really happy?

What kind of things make me really happy when I am surrounded by them?

d) What do other people say about me – what do they give me compliments about – that rings really true to me when I hear these things?

e) Where do I feel I have made a big difference to others and to situations?

f) Where am I being called to make a difference in next?

Take some time to reflect on all of these questions. You may wish to put aside this book for a while and take the time to let these questions sit inside of you. Give space for the light inside of you to emerge fully and speak to you of its presence. Allow this light – your own light – to emerge. And be with it when it does.

Do you see it now? Do you sense it now? Do you feel it now? What is your light saying to you? What is it prompting you to do more of? What does it want you to focus less on? Where does it want you to give yourself more space and take more time for yourself? What does it want you to let go of that in your holding on to, you have blocked your light from emerging? What is it saying to you about you?

When you are with your light, when you are being with your light, there are so many things that it can tell you about you. It can teach you, it can remind you what you are really wise about. You get a soul-deep sensation of 'Hey, I do know this'. Where 'this' is wisdom accumulated through all your past and present life experiences. It can teach you and affirm you to what you already know. Your light tells you to acknowledge that, "Hey, this is what I am really good at." It lets you realize how MUCH you already are. It gives you the realization of how MUCH everything inside of you right now already is.

Allow yourself to be with your light. When someone comes up to you and says, "I really appreciate you for such and such," and they hold your hand and they really mean what they say, be with that and really take it in. Allow yourself to appreciate what they've just said. Stop for a moment all the thoughts of, "Oh, oh, no, no, no this can't be right. No, no, let me give this energy of appreciation that you are putting out at me right back to you. Here, take it back right this instant!" Stop that thought, stop that knee-jerk reaction! Make sure you are really allowing yourself to listen to what they have just said. Allow yourself to take it all in, a hundred-percent, no-holds-barred. That's right, this is you that they're reflecting back at you. They are reflecting your light back at you for you to take in. So take it in this instant.

Mirrors for Self-Reflection of Your Own Light

Whenever you accept wholeheartedly a compliment given to you by someone, your light increases. Whenever you allow yourself to take back in the light that they're reflecting back at you, your internal torch glows even brighter. Notice how people can look so incredibly beautiful when a compliment has been paid at them – that's exactly what happens when they take in their light that's being reflected at them by the person giving them the compliment. They become radiant, they start recognizing themselves for who they are. They start recognizing how brilliant they are. They start recognizing the bright light inside of them. Their light grows and magnifies. And YOU, when you pay them that compliment, help them grow in their light.

So be aware too of the light that other people are putting out into the world. Sometimes, they are not aware of what they are doing. Sometimes, it is a soft glow because they are not fully sure of themselves and part of them is hiding the full extent of their light. And for other people, it is a full-on blaze. They know what they want, they are determined to get it, they are fully proud and confident in what they are standing for, and they do not compromise when they are standing fully in their convictions. They are powerful torches in the world, blazing a powerful trail for all to see and be inspired by. When you see such people, know that that too IS you when you are in your full light. They are your mirror for you to see your own light, for you to see your fullest potential of what you can grow to be, so that you can know truly what it means to be in your own light and OWN your light fully. See yourself in them right now. See yourself in your own mirror right NOW.

Receiving the Activation for the Mirror of Self-Reflection from the Oo-oahnaeriens

The gift that we have for you here is a mirror that reflects back your own light. We are taking this gift and installing it into your field as we speak here. This mirror will assist you in seeing, hearing, knowing and feeling your own light. Breathe as the installation is taking place. Breathe again. Breathe a third time. Feel the mirror entering into places and spaces of your field that you were not even aware of. Feel and sense that light that is being released from your field as the mirror enters into these places and spaces. Be in silence as the mirror enters even more deeply. Listen – what is the mirror saying to you now? What is it telling you about where you are short-changing yourself in terms of how much value and light you are really radiating versus how little of these you believe (mistakenly) yourself to be emanating? What is the mirror making you aware of in terms of your own value as a person – your own value first towards yourself and then towards others as a by-product of this? What does the mirror want you to acknowledge more of about who you are and what you are doing that is so light-filled, that you haven't fully recognized about yourself before? What can you now see about yourself and acknowledge about yourself that is great and wonderful?

Take some time to interact with the mirror. You may imagine the mirror looking at you, right in front of you, being together with you. Ask the mirror the following questions:

a) What do you see about me that you wish to let me know about? Who do you see in me?

b) Where do you see that I am not acknowledging myself enough for who I am?

c) What words of kindness and encouragement would you like to offer me?

d) What would you like me to grow even more into, what would you like me to become MORE of that I already am?

e) What would you like me to fully BE that I already am?

f)   What gifts would you like to draw my attention to that are already present in me?

Let the mirror give you its responses one by one. See, hear, feel or know the mirror speak. Pay attention to each of its answers. Reflect upon each of the answers and write them down as they are, making sure that you are not censoring anything. Then read all the answers again when they have been written down. Let the answers sink into you. Let your light REALLY SINK INTO YOU and integrate with your Being. Let your Being light up with these answers, taking care not to reject any of them.

Congratulations, you have received the activation for realizing your own light. Look into the mirror as often as you can and see what is there for you to realize. Let the mirror reflect back your own light at you and take it all in. Let this happen every single day, every single moment, every single time. You are a blazing bright light and all you need to do is to OWN IT.

Shining Your Light in the World

What are you now going to do with your light? Where are you going to blaze your trail? What matters the most to you now that you know how you are uniquely gifted? Take some time to let these questions sink into your field. We are here supporting you as reflect on these, as you come to your own realizations and make your decisions for where you are committed to blazing your trail. Take care. We will be watching you as you move onward on your path. And we will be supporting you all through your way – whichever your way is, however you choose to express your light to its greatest extent in the world, and whatever choices you make to enable and give yourself the greatest amount of space to be in your own light fully.

Moving to the Final Leg of the Journey

And in the final part of this journey, you will be receiving an activation for getting reconnected back to a deep part of yourself – the part that is always in peace, the part that observes in peace as everything else swirls by, the part of yourself that understands that everything is but an experience that you move through and then let go of. The Kenzohknots are awaiting you in the next chapter, and please feel free to proceed to the last leg of the journey.

Chapter 9

The Activation for Deep Peace of Heart

The Gift of Heart-Song from the Kenzohknots[4]

---

[4] *Note to Readers from Gil: Kensohknots is pronounced 'Ken-swah-nots'.*

W e are the Kenzohknots. We come bearing a gift of gold
for your heart.

The Original Function of Your Heart

Your heart is a precious organ. In its original natural state, it automatically syncs with the rhythms of the Universe, the rhythms of its surroundings, the rhythms of the people who are around you. It has the ability to detect what is around it and to synchronize itself together with all these fields. Very often, it does - so that it can be at one and beat at one with the pulses of everything else in the Universe. It has the ability, through its centre, to be connected to All.

Your heart sings its own song as well. It expresses its joy, its sorrow, its feelings, its desires. It has a desire to be at one with everyone. It has a desire to reach out, and touch. It extends its joyousness and love to all beings regardless of who or what they are.

Your heart is the most precious organ that you have in your being. It makes you human. It makes you flesh and blood. It gives you the capacity to be an infinite source and generator for love. It gives you the capacity for compassion. Your heart makes you extend your love to others and in so doing to welcome them to enter it.

Disturbances of the Heart

And, your heart can also close itself up, or wall itself inside. If there is someone you don't trust, you may decide to close your heart to that person. You may say 'No, I am going to put some distance between myself and them. I don't want this person to come into my heart. This person can hurt me.' You hide behind a wall so you can't be touched even by things and people that would like to touch you positively.

We tell you that when this happens, your heart is not at peace, you are not at peace. While you may attempt to put distance between yourself and the people, things and situations that you don't trust, the fact remains that you are not at peace with them. Your heart is still struggling with the idea of them. It is fighting to keep them away – as far away as possible, so that they cannot come in and stir up the hornets' nest of unresolved issues that you are determinedly stuffing down below the surface of the smooth and cold armor you have put up all around your heart towards the world. While you may pretend that all is well on the surface, beneath in your heart, a tangled knot continues to exist and constrain the way that you love, that way that you express your love, and who you are able to extend your love towards. You start getting selective about who you will allow into your heart, rejecting those who remind you of those experiences in the past where your love was extended and the ridiculed, trampled on, laughed at, or rejected in any number of ways. You close the door of your heart until only a sliver of an entrance remains, accessible only to a select few who have to tiptoe around the landmines that trigger all your fears of being trampled on, hurt, and having your heart destroyed. You close your heart as a default reaction to everyone else who cannot navigate your blockages. You lose the ability to open your heart without condition to All, which your heart in its natural state was designed to be for. You lose the ability to be at one with all other hearts – the ability to touch other people's hearts and to allow them to touch yours.

Restoring your Heart to its Original State

Your heart can be restored to its natural state, which is a state of deep peace. It can be restored to a natural state of deep peace with All of existence. It is the reason for which we are giving you the activation in this chapter. The natural condition of the human heart is to be at peace. It is time for this to be restored into your heart Now.

The Activation for Deep Peace of Heart

The activation for deep peace of heart does a few things. One, it attunes your heart to the natural rhythms of the Universe again. Where you have stored up fear as walls around your heart, the activation allows the rhythms of the Universe to ease past these blocking energies and attune the rhythm of your heart's to the rhythm of the Universe's natural cycles. It gets your heart beating at one once more with ALL.

Two, it dissolves barriers that you have placed around your heart. It eases them away from your heart. It tells these barriers gently that, 'Hey, all is fine. It is okay for you to stand down now.' It brings peace to the parts of you that are still holding on to fear. It tells these fears that all is well and okay now. It soothes fears and makes them feel comfortable enough to stand down.

Lastly, it takes the strength inside of your heart and raises it to whole new levels. It gives the strength of your heart a new voice, a new fire, a whole new reason to come out and express itself powerfully. It tells your heart to GO act on its desires that come truly from the soul via its energetic link to the heart, the desires that are true soul promptings urging the heart to power them into action. It gives your heart a new oomph for it to power your soul-driven choices into material and physical plane manifestations.

Preparing for the Activation

The activation is being prepared for you as you read through this next paragraphs. Before it is given to you, it is necessary for you to open yourself up to receiving it. You may do this by taking a pen and some paper and writing down the following in a reflection exercise. Reflect on and write down:

a) One thing that you really really want to do.

b) One thing that you really really do not want to do. Something that causes you consternation to do, that you yet feel obliged to do at the present time. Something that you would chuck out of your field right away if you had the choice.

c) One thing that you really really want for a person that you care about or love. It could be a gift that you really want for them to receive, something that you know is going to be impactful for them and touch them deeply. A gift of love that you want to give to them - from the bottommost of your heart.

d) One thing that you would like to receive from someone you love. These could be words of encouragement from the person that you know are truly going to touch you. Or an affirmation of you that lets you know that someone truly gets what you are going through and does take you to their heart. Anything that you really want to receive into the bottom of your heart where it will be cherished and valued dearly.

e) One thing that you want to give out to the world. This could be words that bring across a heartfelt message to the world and tell the world of the deep feelings that you have towards it, and a heartfelt blessing that you wish for the world. It could also be a gift that you would like to give to the world – something that is special about you, something you are really really good at doing or being that you want to bring out more of to the world.

f) One thing you want the world to acknowledge you for that would touch your heart greatly. This could be a message that you wish to receive/hear from the world if it could speak in a collective voice. Something that would bring you comfort and let you know that the world sees and accepts all of you as you are – all of you, every single part of you, warts and all.

Write each of these things down on your sheet of paper. Feel each of them stirring in your heart when you are done. Where in your life are you delaying yourself from taking action to move forward with these things that are mattering to you? Where have you stopped yourself from asking to receive the energies and words and gifts that you would like to receive from the parties that matter to you? Ask yourself these two critical questions. And then start writing down where you can begin taking action to give and receive that which matters to you. Enjoy yourself during this process of realizing what you haven't been putting attention to that does matter to you, and enjoy yourself as you go through the process of making the new commitments to yourself to getting them done.

Receiving the Activation for Deep Peace of Heart

And now, you are ready for the activation. Close your eyes, please. Close your eyes, and imagine yourself sinking into your heart. Inside of your heart, there is a spot that feels like a sacred, safe space. Walk into this place. Be in this place. And then from this place, hear a song arising from the depths of your heart. Hear the song emerge from this sacred space. Go even deeper into the song and merge with it, becoming at one with it. Hear what the song has to say to you. Listen to its lyrics. Listen to its whispers. Listen to it tell you of all that is real and true about you. Thank it for giving you its truth. Clasp the hands of the song, and bow towards it.

And congratulations, you have received the gift of the song of your heart. What has the heart-song told you about you? Where are you now wanting to take more action to express the truth of the song of your heart in your life? Let your heart speak to you on this as its own song emerges and takes the center-stage of your life. Make a commitment to listen to your heart more often, to give your heart voice. Let it speak so that you can do and be what matters and therefore be at peace with what is. Listening to your heart is the key to your peace for your entire life.

The entire series of 7 activations has been designed to reconnect you with yourself. When you listen to your heart, it tells you what it needs and what it wants you to do so that you may be at peace with yourself. It tells you where you need to take action that you have been avoiding. It gives you the motivation to start and to keep going. It tells you where you need to stop to honour your own boundaries and make sure that you are giving yourself time and space for yourself – time and space for You to be YOU.

Your Heart as the Key to Finding YOU

Your heart is the key to many things in life. Use it wisely to navigate through life. Make use of its capabilities, its functions, and its desires. Use it to tell you how to move and where to go. Above all, listen to it tell you of who you are not and hence who you really are. It cannot fail you, because this IS the function it was designed for.

Your heart is awaiting an even greater connection with You.

Congratulations on the end of the Journey

And this concludes the entire series of 7 activations from all of us 7 star races! We rejoice and congratulate you on having undertaken the entire journey with commitment, courage, motivation, and strong personal desire to reach the goal of finding and being yourself.

In the next and final chapter, the galactic team for Starseed support would like to give you some concluding blessings and benedictions. They await you there. Please go onwards to the next chapter to receive their final words and to allow yourself to be honoured and celebrated for the journey that you have completed in this book. You have done well.

Chapter 10

The Conclusion of this Journey, and What's Next?

Congratulations on reaching this point in the journey. You have done so much. It was not easy reaching this point. For some of you, this was an uncomfortable process. You had to take a look at things you preferred to deny. You are confronted by parts of yourself that you found very challenging. Every single thing has happened for a reason. And sometimes, that reason is not what you expect, and this is now only becoming to become more and more apparent to you. Yes, you realize it now. These are all YOU. Whatever that has happened is the making of YOU. It is all good. You will realize even more of this in time to come.

What's Next?

What are you going to do now? Where have new plans formed in your life after reading this book and reflecting on yourself? What is the most important thing for you right now? Tell us. Write to us about these matters. We will read what you write. We will assist you with manifesting your goals. Place what you have written inside an envelope. Seal the envelope. Then say a prayer over it as follows:

I wish all the best to all of my endeavours, to all of myself, to all that I am. This is Me. It is all me. And this I accept. I will honour all of me. Amen – so it is, it so is.

You may give this envelope to us. Simply set the intention for the contents of the envelope to travel up to us. We will read it. We will be assisting in coordinating the things that are needed for you to manifest your goals, or to bring you greater clarity, or to suggest different directions to better get you aligned with that which your soul is directing for you. Open a channel to us. Seek us out. We stand in support of you. It is important work what each and every one of you has undertaken at the level of soul for planet Earth. It is important that you receive support. RECEIVE it from us. We will bring it to you.

More From Us

When you are ready, more from us will come. You will get assignments. It will be what you like to do. You will receive downloads and messages from us. You will like what you see. Enjoy this.

And with this, we now leave you. Contact Gil if you wish to learn more. She has some more downloads for all of you. She will be distributing packages of care and reconnections for all of you. She has more to offer all of you. We are all waiting, with all our love.

The Galactic Coordination Team for Earth Starseed Reactivation and Support, together with Gil Sim

Also Check Out

Higher Purpose Activation
Galactic Cards Deck

These cards contain portals, energies and keys that remind you of your mission and purpose in relation to the entire cosmos, and in the grander scheme of the evolution of human consciousness. Use these cards to Get On Purpose and Keep Going! Each card contains powerful downloads that remind you of why you are here and helps you ground Divine inspirations and downloads from the higher realms into useful forms on the physical plane (e.g. products and services) that benefit those on the Earth community you have come to be of service to.

Order now at http://www.cosmic-light-human.com

A Teaching from the Mayans

12-Strand DNA Anchoring and Restructuring
DNA Level 1 Class

Discover what the Mayans knew about the secrets of human DNA in this phenomenal multi-day class. Learn powerful methods for clearing your DNA of old ancestral stuff that is weighing down your ascension into finer vibratory rates and for bringing new light into your genes. Use these tools for yourself and for service to others.

RRP: US$1,100

More information at

http://www.cosmic-light-human.com/DNALevel1